THE JOY OF SUFFERING

ISBN: 9798674836223

A Publication of Tall Pine Books || tallpinebooks.com

*Printed in the United States of America

THE JOY OF SUFFERING

MARK MOROZOV

TALL PINE
BOOKS

CONTENTS

FOREWORD

Suffering carries a unique responsibility in the life of a believer in Jesus. Jesus is our pattern. Jesus is God's blueprint for our lives. All of us that love Him are currently being conformed to His image, and suffering is one of the beautiful tools that God uses in order to raise up a powerful people that look like His Son in the earth.

Jesus said it best Himself, "The Son of Man must suffer many things..."(Luke 9:22) The writer of Hebrews gives us the profound statements about Jesus by saying, "In the days of His flesh, He offered up both prayers and supplications with loud crying and tears to the One that was able to save Him from death, and He was heard because of His piety. Although He was a

Son, He learned obedience from the things that He suffered." (Hebrews 5:7-8)

Let us consider it this way. If Jesus is our blueprint and our being conformed to His image is God's goal for our lives, and He had to suffer many things, and God used those many things in order to perform and perfect His purposes, then we can rest assured that suffering is going to be a valuable piece of our experience while we have days that are to be lived out in the flesh.

Paul said it best when he was speaking from his own heart and life when he said, "that I might know Him and the power of His resurrection and the fellowship of His sufferings..." (Philippians 3:10) Paul is giving us insight into the beautiful reality that there is a fellowship with Jesus that can be known through suffering. And in some instances, there is a fellowship with Jesus that can only be known through suffering.

There is something wonderful about suffering that serves God's desire to absolve us from the self-dependent life that many too often live. The strength of our own wants and ways are at times much to fierce. We have become proficient in providing all of the proper externals in order to look and sound like we are really dependent on God, when in actuality, we have done nothing except perfected our own religiosity which has all of the right images and filters, yet is sourced by a love of self and a desire to satisfy all of our own demands.

It is here that the consideration of Jesus and His suffering becomes paramount. The psalmist writes prophetically, "I delight to do your will..." (Psalm 40:8) The potential to have delight in the midst of hardship is real. The ability to have peace that surpasses all understanding is real. (Philippians 4:7) The possibility to have joy when there is pain, tragedy, and sorrow, is real. Whether through pruning or persecution His joy can be made complete in our lives. (John 15:11)

Lovers of Jesus, hear this clearly—you can attempt to spend the rest of your life avoiding suffering. But if you choose this path you may also in fact find yourself in moments directly avoiding the will of God.

Paul, in Romans, speaks loud and clear to our hearts in saying, "if we are children, heirs also, heirs of God and fellow heirs with Christ, if indeed we suffer with Him so that we may also be glorified with Him." (Romans 8:17)

Jesus is the suffering servant who has been glorified forever. Praise God! And we too, through suffering, are bringing glory to God as He is working all things together for good to those that love Him and are called according to His purpose. (Romans 8:28)

I believe that what Mark has written for us that you are going to encounter in the pages to follow is an injection of life and perspective to those of us who love Him so that we can live faithfully for the Lord and be everything that He has dreamed of our lives being. We want to be pleasing to Jesus, and this book is going to help you do that by helping you to create the proper perspective about some of the most difficult moments and seasons that life will have to offer.

Jesus is worthy of a people that would love Him and love Him well. And there is no better way to say I love you than to lay down your life. May you lay your life down for the King and be filled to overflowing with His resurrection power working in you as you find joy in suffering!

—MICHAEL DOW

Founder & Director, *Burning Ones*

CONTENTS

INTRODUCTION

As I started to write this book, little did I know what I was about to step into. I knew the Lord had called me to write for over a year and a half. The thought of it would not leave my mind. I know there are some really good books out there on suffering, so I didn't understand why I needed to write something like this. It wasn't until I reached the last chapter that I realized how perfect the Lord's timing is. As I come to finish writing this book, the whole world has come to a standstill—what they call a *pandemic* has hit the earth, and every nation has closed its borders. It might not have hit home for you just yet, but it will.

I remember going into KFC one day and asking the cashier what she thought of this whole pandemic. She answered, "It has not hit me yet." What will we do when it does hit people? Many will lose their jobs, houses will be foreclosed, cars will be repossessed, and many will come into a season of turmoil, pain, and suffering. What to do in the midst of all of this? What now? Many are asking if this is the end, but I believe it's just the beginning. The closer we come to the last days, the more what we read in the Book of Revelation will come into fulfillment in our lifetime.

I can now see that this is the perfect book for the perfect time. Little did I know that everything was in the Lord's timing. Many times I felt a filling of the Holy Spirit—a breathing of His presence—as I opened the Bible and read, and began to write. I pray and believe that as you open these pages and journey through this book, you will be blessed by the visitation of His presence, the visitation of His comfort, and the visitation of His joy.

There are many theological books on suffering which look at many questions. Is suffering from the Lord or from the enemy? Why does God allow suffering? If it's not from Him, why would God allow suffering if He's good? Why did a relative die? Why did a tragedy hit my life? Why these financial problems? Was the coronavirus from God? Was it God's judgment that hit the earth with COVID-19?

I'm sure many of these questions are running through your mind, and I believe that there are answers for them all. But this isn't a theological book to give you all the answers for suffering in your life. Instead, it's a book to point to the joy you can have in the midst of your suffering.

Jesus Himself said you will have suffering. But He will not leave you alone. He'll walk with you through it all because He has overcome it all. As you read this book, my heart is to help you experience the joy given by Jesus and the comfort He offers to get you through this season of your life. He has promised comfort and joy in our suffering if we will receive them from Him.

As you read this book, I pray that you will receive the revelation of why you must have joy in the midst of it all. As I have been writing this book for the last year and a half, the Lord has led me through a season of suffering that I can't even talk about just yet. But in the midst of it I have found a joy that is given only by the Lord, only by the comfort of His Holy Spirit, only by the manifest presence of Jesus. I am believing for an anointing of joy in the midst of your trials. I am believing for a shift of seasons and that as you read these pages, you will begin to experience visitations of the Lord in seemingly random moments throughout your suffering.

May the name of the Lord Jesus Christ be exalted through this book!

THE REALITY OF THE CHRISTIAN LIFE

THIS WAS where the journey began.

I was sitting in a hospital bed in what felt like the middle of nowhere, all of a sudden struck with the truth that life is much shorter than I had realized. I was starting to see that there had to be a bigger purpose to this thing we call *life*, especially if God was allowing me to go through the pain I was experiencing.

I loved God, and I knew that He was the One who had sent me there, but it was hard for me to understand how I could face that kind of suffering when I knew Him to be an all-loving Father, One who would protect me. Really, I was dumbfounded. It felt like everything I had ever known was being shaken. But in the midst of it all, I was able to stand on the one thing that I knew for sure: God works everything for the good of those who love Him and are called according to His purpose.[1]

I had never planned to travel to India, but I felt an urge in my heart to go on mission. It didn't really matter where I went; I just knew that God was calling me to *go* and preach the Gospel. So I approached my church leaders and asked if there were any upcoming opportunities to go on mission overseas, and they suggested I travel with a team to India. I immediately agreed.

A few weeks later, I was on a plane flying to Bangalore with great anticipation. During this trip, our team travelled to different locations where we preached the Gospel and helped strengthen the local churches, along with organizing a few street crusades. It was an amazing experience, and God was moving powerfully through the team. But for me, there came a sudden turning point: I became sick with dengue fever two weeks before I was supposed to fly back home.

I was admitted to a Catholic hospital in a small village, and I hadn't felt well for over a week. I felt weaker than ever before, and the pain was worse than I can describe—I have had my share of pain before, but this was far worse than anything I'd experienced. It felt as if mosquitoes were eating my body, like my feet and hands were under a hot flame, and like my head was being beaten by a baseball bat. I had significant nerve pain, and my stomach...oh boy, my stomach!

I remember walking over to the stairwell on the side of the hospital building one morning around 2:30a.m. Because my hands felt like they were on fire, I held on to the metal guardrails to try to cool them down. With tears streaming down my face, I cried out to God, "Why?! Why?!"

He spoke to me in a still, small voice: "You wanted Me to use you; I must get you ready."

"Why does it have to be so hard?" I asked.

He answered, "It's through the fire that I can mold and shape you."

He wasn't saying that He had caused the sickness —I believe sickness is from the enemy—but simply that He was going to use the suffering to prepare me for what was ahead in my future.

It was at that moment I remembered all the prayers I had previously brought before the Lord. I thought of one occasion, two years earlier, when I had been praying in a field close to my home. The lights began to turn off, and I was the only one left in the park. *I'll pray just a few more minutes*, I thought. Getting on my knees, I cried out to the Lord, "Use me, Lord. I know I am not able, but You are. Take my life if

You will not use it." Little did I know what I was signing up for.

A few minutes later, while I was still praying, I looked up and saw two men wearing masks approaching me from the woods. They were heading straight in my direction. Behind me was a lake and more woods. The spirit of fear hit me. I felt like I had to run, but my car was on the other side of these two men. So I had two choices: run and scream, or stand my ground and stand on the Lord as my refuge in time of need. I began to worship and pray in tongues, battling with fear as I did, praying fervently in the Spirit. I looked up and saw these men still approaching with their heads and faces covered. I remembered what I had just said to the Lord about Him taking my life, so I thought, *This is it.*

I was praying in tongues, knowing the Bible says that when we pray in the Spirit, we edify ourselves. As I did, I began to be filled with the Holy Spirit, knowing I could not get out of this on my own. The men approached me and walked right by without saying a word, as if I had completely disappeared from sight. As they walked farther and farther away, I got up and walked back to my car, worshipping God. As soon as I got inside the car, I grabbed my Bible and opened it only to see Isaiah 51:12 highlighted before me. I began to read as if it were God Himself speaking to me.

> "I, even I, am He who comforts you. Who are you that you should be afraid of a man who will die, and of the son of a man who will be made like grass? And you forget the Lord your Maker, who stretched out the heavens and laid the foundations of the earth; you have feared continually every day because of the fury of the oppressor, when he has prepared to destroy. And where is the fury of the oppressor? The captive exile hastens, that he may be loosed, that he should not die in the pit, and that his bread should not fail. But I am the Lord your God, who divided the sea whose waves roared —the Lord of hosts is His name. And I have put My words in your mouth; I have covered you with the shadow of My hand, that I may plant the heavens, lay the foundations of the earth, and say to Zion, 'You are My people.'"
>
> ISAIAH 51:12–16

"I am He who comforts you," He said to me. "Who are you to fear these men, who are like grass? I am the Lord your God, your Maker, who made the earth and is over the earth." This vivid memory came back to me as I stood in the hospital stairwell in India in tremendous pain. In my suffering, I remembered that my God is over all! Right away, He spoke something to me that changed my life forever:

"Mark, you will be healed. When you go home, I don't want you to go back to your job and the lifestyle you had before."

"What should I do?" I asked Him.

"Seek My face."

A day or two later, I received a phone call from a man in Africa who prophesied that I would be healed, confirming what God had spoken to me. I received this word by faith, believing God for my healing. Not long after, our team's main contact on the trip, Pastor Morris, picked me up and drove me to a better hospital in the city of Bangalore. When I arrived there, I was attended by several doctors who tried to put needles into my veins to pump fluid through my body, since I was so dehydrated from the dengue fever. They were struggling to find my veins, so they began to poke around my skin with the needles. I can't describe the torture I went through. I was sure at that time that if persecution felt like anything, this was it! After a while, the doctors were still unsuccessful, because my wrists and arms were so swollen from all the previous needles. In the end, they had to put a needle they use for babies in through my hand.

I was scheduled to return home to the United States in a few days' time, but Pastor Morris and others encouraged me to stay in the hospital longer, reminding me that I had insurance which would cover all of the medical costs. Honestly, I just wanted to get out of there and return home to my comfortable bed, enjoy a hot shower, and forget any of this ever happened. But I also knew God was going to heal me. I had to tell the team, "No, I'll still go home when I'm supposed to."

RECOVERY & TRAINING

The next day, a young man I had never met came to the hospital and brought a strange concoction for me to drink made of papaya leaves. This was the most extreme taste I have ever experienced! Holding my nose, I poured the papaya-leaf smoothie into my mouth and swallowed it. I drank it again in the afternoon, hoping that it would help alleviate my suffering, although previously, drinking papaya juice had only seemed to make things worse. However, the next day, my platelet count began to rise and I started feeling a little better.

God is faithful!

I began to quickly recover, and two days later, I was discharged from the hospital and preparing to fly back home. I still had some trouble walking, so I was supposed to be moved around in a wheelchair. The following day, it was almost time to go, and remarkably, for the first time in two weeks, I was hungry. I sat at a table with Pastor Morris and his wife, Oksana, the couple who had organized the program for our trip, along with some other guests. All they gave me to eat was a plate of white rice, but I looked across the table and saw some cooked chicken, so I reached over and grabbed several pieces, tossing them onto my plate with a smile on my face. Pastor Oksana reached back over and took the chicken away from me, saying, "Are you crazy?!" I hadn't eaten in two weeks, so she assumed the chicken would mess up my stomach. I was a little angry with her, wondering what kind of person would deny me a piece of chicken! So I thought to myself, *In a few hours, I will be back in the States and will be able to eat a fat steak! Yes, I said it, a fat steak!*

When we arrived at the airport to depart from India, I felt like I had never been sick. After we landed in the States, I ordered a small pizza and ate it (which was probably not the smartest idea given all the grease it had, and the fact that I had only eaten two meals before this). I was satisfied and happy. God had healed me! For the next few days, I relaxed at home, slept around twelve hours a day, and thoroughly rested.

Having fully recovered, it was time for my real mission to begin: commencing with my training. I remembered what God had spoken to me in that hospital stairwell—to *seek* Him. So I began with what Matthew 6:33 says: "But seek first the kingdom of God and His righteousness, and all these things shall be added to you." I had to give myself first to seeking the Kingdom of heaven, not going back to the regular life I had before.

Previously, I had been working overtime every week for a purpose that was earthly, one that was eating away at my time. My Christian life was lukewarm and lifeless. I went to work and to church. I was an usher at church. I did all the "church things" that seemed to be the right thing at the time. I would put a smile on at church, but at home, I was miserable. I would pray two times a week, each time spending five minutes asking God for things to check off my list, thinking this was all the Christian life was meant to be. I was blind to the fact that I was blind.

I believe the worst place you can be is in the midst of a problem without knowing there's a problem. It's always easy to fix a leak on a boat when it's small, but the longer you leave it open, the more water will continue streaming through the hole until it gets bigger and bigger and eventually, like the Titanic, it sinks. I was leaking and did not know it. I was playing the "church" game.

But now I had a mandate from God. *Seek My face.* And as I did, these worldly attitudes and behaviors began to fade away, replaced by the fire of intimacy with Jesus. I began to do the very things we're all called to do: sit at the feet of Jesus, grow in intimate relationship with Him, and understand the price He paid for us. As I began to know Him more, I started understanding myself and my purpose here on this earth. True identity began to manifest in my life, and things slowly began to change.

My old boss, who happened to be my brother, offered me my old job back with an extra fifty percent on top of what I had previously earned—a deal that no reasonable person would refuse. I managed his business and was in charge of a crew of thirteen employees; he had started a new business and was handing full control to me. I was also doing side jobs selling cars, like most Russians. But I knew what would happen if I went back to this job. I would be enticed back to the old me, to my old lukewarm lifestyle. Some are called to impact the work sphere, but deep inside, I knew there was something else for me, and if I went back, I would not be in the full purpose and will of the Father. So I told him I was sorry, that

God had given me a bigger purpose and a higher calling that I had to follow.

VISION & CALLING

In this new season, I became aware of the calling God had placed on my life. It wasn't something completely new, but rather, had been birthed in me years before.

I received a vision at a conference in 2013 in which I saw myself standing on a stage with several hundred people in front of me. Initially, I thought it was pride that was causing me to "see" this, but really, it was a glimpse of the future God had for me. I knew I was the one in the vision, but I didn't know how it could possibly happen—I was no speaker or preacher. I remember when I was in college and was asked to do a presentation in front of fifteen people, and I was so scared of speaking in front of groups that I didn't come into class that week. On another occasion, I sat at a bonfire with a friend, Daniel, who asked me, "Mark, what is it you want to do in life?" I said I wasn't sure, but that I saw myself standing in front of a crowd overseas.

A year later, I shared this vision with a group of my leader friends—so I thought—and they laughed at me. This broke me on the inside and threw me into turmoil, having just begun to believe this was possibly a vision from God. But I gave in to doubt because I never saw it in myself to be the preacher in the vision.

I wanted to go into business; this is what I saw for my life. My brothers are businessmen, so I was going to be one, as well. This was all I had aimed for in life: to be a businessman and have nice things. It was my purpose. Occasionally, I would give in and call that my mission. I actually had a stronger income coming in then than I do now, and I give two, if not three times more to the Great Commission now than I did then. It is my joy to be a blessing to our generation and the Great Commission. Honestly, I can say now that I was lukewarm before I went to India, but I definitely did not think so then.

During my time in India, I was given an opportunity to share my testimony at a crusade. Testifying on that stage, I remembered the vision I had received two years earlier. This was it! This was the exact vision I saw. People had laughed at the vision, but here I was witnessing its fulfillment.

God is faithful, friends. He wants to give you a vision for your life, and He is determined to accomplish it. Once you have faith and obey His

"It's when you begin to abide in Him that your desires become His desires."

voice, the dreams He places inside of you will be fulfilled. The Bible says, "Delight yourself also in the

Lord, and He shall give you the desires of your heart."[2] It's when you begin to abide in Him that your desires become His desires. As the light shines, the darkness is removed and motives become clean and pure. He places *His* vision inside your heart, and as you obey, He will bring it to pass.

What God began in my life was too precious to give away for earthly possessions—money, success, and possessions that will just burn up like everything else in this world. Life on earth is here today and gone tomorrow. Jesus said, "The harvest truly is plentiful, but the laborers are few. Therefore pray the Lord of the harvest to send out laborers into His harvest."[3] If Jesus said the harvest was plentiful during His time on earth, how much more plentiful is it now?

God is looking for people He can place His vision inside. Will you run with the vision God has given you, just as Nehemiah did when he returned to Jerusalem to rebuild its walls, regardless of the opposition you may face? He is waiting for you, and the vision will only be accomplished if you abide in Him and obey Him. He has a big plan for your life.

It's not worth selling out for a few coins like Judas did when he betrayed Jesus for thirty pieces of silver. Because at the end of the day, you can't take your car or your house to heaven. You only take yourself and other people. My greatest joy when I get to heaven will not be the things I did on the earth; it will be the souls that are there because of something that God did through my life. Souls, souls, salvation of souls— this is the greatest joy one can experience.

Following Jesus is much more than coming to an altar. It's much more than simply saying, "Use me, Lord." It means picking up your cross and following Him. It's to deny self, to deny culture, even to deny family at times. It's to die to yourself and do whatever the Father tells you to do, just as Jesus did.

To follow God is a life of sacrifice. It's a life of brokenness at times, and many people will misunderstand you. It's to be an outsider, to go through the narrow gate and not the wide. But despite all of this, there is no better place to be than exactly where the Lord has called you. That might be overseas, in another state, in your own city, at school, at a job, or in a career. I know many people who are sent by God as missionaries to their workplaces, schools, and local communities. The important thing is to be where *He* wants you to be.

Some of us have become cold and inactive in our calling. We say that we are *called* to give financially, yet we cannot even give a ten-percent tithe to our local church. We say we are *called* as a teacher or preacher, yet we have never shared the Gospel with anyone. We say we are *called* to serve God in business but focus on ourselves, driving expensive cars and only feeding our flesh. But God has so much more for you than the routine of your job, family, and church attendance. The very thing you need can only be found in one place: the secret place. As you spend time seeking the Lord, everything else He desires for you will begin to be fulfilled. It begins and ends in His presence.

Maybe you are not sharing the Gospel with your neighbor because you're afraid. It's God's presence that drives all fear away. Maybe you find it too hard to give at least ten percent of your finances. It's in His presence that you become a lover of Him, not of materialistic possessions or status.

Maybe you do not know what His will is for your life. It's first to be *with* Him that you were called. I am confident that God has brought

> "The very thing you need can only be found in one place: *the secret place.*"

you here so that you might become intimate with Him. And by "here," I mean the very pages of this book, and the place you sit now as you read. This was the beginning for me. As I began to pray, fast, and seek the face of God, He revealed more clearly the calling He had for my life. And in the secret place, I began to intimately know the One who would walk beside me as I lived out this calling, through the good times and in the suffering.

"*He* is our exceedingly great reward."

The road ahead was never going to be easy—He never promised a smooth life —but it was (and is) going to be worth it all at the end of the day. I could have avoided the suffering by choosing a comfortable, prosperous life, but I would have missed *Him*. And *He* is our exceedingly great reward.[4]

A MAN OF GOD

God does not call us down an easy road. Sometimes the people who seem to have the greatest calling are also the ones who experience the most suffering. The Bible is full of stories of men and women of God who accomplished great things yet suffered greatly. There is an enemy out there, and he is not happy with you taking his property and bringing people to the cross. *The spiritual is more real than the natural we see today.*

The Apostle Paul was one of those who suffered for the Gospel. We know Paul as the man who saw many miracles, healings, and salvations, but he was also a man of suffering; before his conversion, he was the cause of it for so many Christians who were perse-cuted and killed for their faith in Jesus.

The Bible says that Paul (also called Saul) "made havoc of the church, entering every house, and dragging off men and women, committing them to prison"[5] and that he was "breathing threats and murder against the disciples of the Lord."[6] He was a man you didn't want to mess with! But one day, he had an encounter with Jesus that completely changed his life. You probably know the story well.

> "As he journeyed he came near Damascus, and suddenly a light shone around him from heaven.
>
> Then he fell to the ground, and heard a voice saying to him, 'Saul, Saul, why are you persecuting Me?' And he said, 'Who are You, Lord?'
>
> Then the Lord said, 'I am Jesus, whom you are persecuting. It is hard for you to kick against the goads.'"
>
> ACTS 9:3–5

Remember, when others persecute you, they are really persecuting Jesus. That's what Jesus told Saul in this encounter. He is with you in all your suffering, feeling the same pain that you feel. And it hurts Him to see His people suffer, even when He knows the suffering will produce good fruit.

When Saul arose from this encounter with Jesus, he was blind. His companions led him into the city, and the Bible says, "He was three days without sight, and neither ate nor drank."[7] Talk about an introduction to Christianity! This wasn't comfortable and easygoing like many of us hope our lives will be. While Saul was still blind, God spoke to a man named Ananias to go and pray for Saul to receive his sight. The very last thing the Lord said to Ananias was, "I will show [Saul] how many things he must suffer for My name's sake."[8] Saul was marked with the sufferings of Christ before his ministry ever began.

After he was healed, Paul began to preach that Jesus was the Son of God, to the amazement of those who knew him as a terrorizer of Christians. This incredible transformation was obvious to everyone, and it would result in his first experience of suffering for the Gospel. "Now after many days were past, the Jews plotted to kill him."[9] I doubt many of us faced that kind of opposition so early in our walk with Jesus. What a whirlwind experience this was for Saul —he had just been saved, started preaching the Gospel, and was already being persecuted.

Later on in his ministry, Paul and his companion Silas were locked up in prison for following Jesus. It would seem they had every reason to be downcast and joyless—but instead, they chose joy in their suffering. They prayed and sang hymns to God. The next time you face hardship for the sake of Jesus, reject the temptation to complain and start singing praises to God. The result was dramatic: a huge earthquake shook the prison, all the doors flung open, and every prisoner's chains were loosed.

And that wasn't even the end of it—the jailer, who was about to commit suicide, received the Gospel, and his entire family was saved and baptized. Paul and Silas had been beaten and impris-

> **"The next time you face hardship for the sake of Jesus, reject the temptation to complain, and start singing praises to God."**

oned, but they knew the end result was that Jesus would be glorified and they would come out on top.

If you are persecuted for the sake of the Gospel, you will come out on top in Jesus' name!

Whatever you are walking through, you will see the victory in Jesus' name!

Paul also received prophetic words that would scare many of us. One prophet named Agabus tied his own hands and feet with Paul's belt and said, "Thus says the Holy Spirit, 'So shall the Jews at Jerusalem bind the man who owns this belt, and deliver him into the hands of the Gentiles.'"[10] Imagine receiving that word! In spite of this warning, Paul continued on to Jerusalem to fulfill the mission God had given him, saying, "I am ready not only to be bound, but also to die at Jerusalem for the name of the Lord Jesus."[11]

This generation loves the acronym YOLO—You

Only Live Once—the idea that we should live life to the fullest. Paul lived his life to the fullest for Jesus, unafraid to suffer or even die. When you are scared of what people think about you or might do to you, you can never accomplish the complete will of the Father. Instead, fear will drive you to serve the will of man. When you fear God, you live before Him; you are unafraid and understand who is really King in your life. When Jesus is your King and Lord, suffering turns into glory, because you understand that bigger things are coming your way. It's a joy to walk through hardships when you know what is on the other side. This was what drove Paul to continue his mission with joy—he understood the end result.

As a result of his suffering, Paul had many opportunities to preach the Gospel and share his testimony: to the Jews in Jerusalem, before the religious council, in front of Felix the governor and King Agrippa, and on the island of Malta. In Malta, after a catastrophic shipwreck, the devil tried to attack Paul with a snake that came out of the firewood and bit him. But it could not stop God's plans for the people. Life will throw snakes at you during times of trial and hardship, but remember, God puts nothing to waste and causes everything to turn for the good. The power of God was released through Paul, and every sick person on the island was healed. The same hand that was bitten by the snake ended up healing the sick.

Paul's life was marked by suffering from beginning to end, but through it all, he was able to find joy in the Lord, through the power of the Holy Spirit.

EMBRACING SUFFERING

"If I must boast, I will boast of the things that show my weakness."

2 CORINTHIANS 11:30 (NIV)

This is a very countercultural statement from Paul. People boasted then, and they boast today. But this kind of boasting looks a little different. Even though he was a very educated and influential man, Paul chose to boast in his sufferings and weaknesses.

He knew that when he was weak, he was strong. It was a joy for him to suffer for Christ, and he knew that in his weakness, he would have

"God puts nothing to waste and causes everything to turn for the good."

the privilege of experiencing the power of God resting upon him. He knew this because Jesus had said to Paul, "My grace is sufficient for you, for my power is made perfect in weakness."[12] What was Paul's response? "Therefore I will boast all the more gladly about my weaknesses, so that Christ's power may rest on me. That is why, for Christ's sake, I delight in weaknesses, in insults, in hardships, in persecutions, in difficulties. For when I am weak, then I am strong."[13]

Can you say that about yourself, that you delight in weakness? How about insults? Hardships? Persecution? It's only possible to be joyful in these things when you know the reality of the

> **"I delight in weaknesses, in insults, in hardships, in persecutions, in difficulties. For when I am weak, then I am strong."**

power of God that can rest upon you. Paul was ready to take on the perfect will of God for his life because he was able to embrace the suffering. He received comfort from the Holy Spirit and had joy because he had a true revelation of suffering. He knew what it meant to partake in Christ, not just through prayer, but also through suffering.

> "In fact, everyone who wants to live a godly life in Christ Jesus will be persecuted."
>
> 2 TIMOTHY 3:12 (NIV)

Suffering may come in many forms, but one of

these—persecution—is not just a possibility; it is a promise from God. It is promised to all of us who want to live a godly life, and a promise for all who sacrifice for the Kingdom. Jesus told His disciples that by giving up family and property for His sake and the sake of the Gospel, they would receive a hundredfold blessing.[14] But in the same verse, He also promised persecution. The valley—persecution—is real, but so is the mountain—a hundredfold blessing. If this kind of suffering is guaranteed, we should choose to embrace it and receive the full revelation of how God wants to use it for our blessing.

Many godly men and women throughout history have faced persecution far greater than you or I have. All of the Apostles, except for John, were killed for their faith. Peter was crucified upside down because he refused to die in the same way as his Lord. Stephen, the first martyr, was stoned to death by the Jewish religious leaders for following Jesus, but in his final moments, he was filled with joy as he saw Jesus standing at the right hand of the Father in heaven.

King David said, "Even though I walk through the darkest valley, I will fear no evil, for you are with me; your rod and your staff, they comfort me."[15] There are times in life when it feels like we have ascended the mountain of God and every problem has disappeared from view. At other times, the valley seems so deep we cannot figure out how we will ever escape it. No matter which season you are in, you can have fullness of joy as you abide in His presence. Throughout this book, I want you to see the purpose and blessing of suffering in your life, so that no matter what comes your way, you can have this joy.

2

THE PURPOSE OF SUFFERING

AS LONG AS we are on this earth, we will face hardships. I wrote this book to help you understand the purpose suffering has in your life, and the joy you can find in the midst of it. Many people ask, is suffering from God? When they see suffering in the world around them, they think it is evidence that there cannot be a *good* God. How could a good God allow these things to happen? You will surely encounter opposition and affliction at some point, but God isn't necessarily the source of these things. Instead, He allows you to experience hardships for a reason. In the midst of light, there is a little bit of darkness to prove that the light is there.

I don't believe that God is the source of all our suffering. Remember, it's the enemy who steals, kills, and destroys. [1]People die all the time; they get sick; they face traumatic circumstances. But consider the blind man in John 9. Jesus reveals that this man's ailment was not due to some personal or family sin, but so that the *glory of God* could be revealed through his healing. God did not make this man blind, but He turned the situation around to bring glory to Himself; He had a purpose for the suffering. Things are not always as they seem, and it's not our job to figure it all out. We just need to trust in the purposes of God for our lives.

Sometimes we can see how God might use our suffering for good, but it still causes us to be in despair. The problem is that many of us don't fully understand the Kingdom of God. We think that suffering is connected with sadness, and that only when the suffering is over will we find our joy again. But the Kingdom is completely different than this.

When Jesus died on the cross, He accomplished many things on our behalf. Of course, His death first paid for the forgiveness of our sins, but it also opened the way for the Holy Spirit to dwell within each of us. Only a clean vessel could receive God on the inside. The Bible says that "the kingdom of God is... righteousness and peace and joy in the Holy Spirit."[2] And we know joy is the second fruit of the Holy Spirit listed in Galatians 5:22. Therefore, because of His death and the coming of the Holy Spirit, Jesus has ensured that we can have joy in the midst of suffering. As we enter into the reality of Jesus' Kingdom, we know that we will face trials, because He promised them to us. When we do, it's important that we allow God to accomplish His purposes for us through these tests.

The enemy will try to make our life hell. Remember his goal: to steal, kill, and destroy. He wants to steal our peace and joy, kill our hopes and dreams, and destroy the trust we have in God. He knows we are a threat to his kingdom when we are following Jesus and fulfilling the calling on our lives. As this opposition arises, we have the choice to follow Jesus and trust His grace for our trials, knowing that He will use them to make us stronger and more like Himself.

But suffering can also be caused by our own bad choices. Sometimes we blame the devil for our problems when we are responsible for the pit we have

> "As we enter into the reality of Jesus' Kingdom, we know that we will face trials because He promised them to us."

fallen into. There are consequences for our actions; sin leads to death. Perhaps you are blaming the devil for the suffering that you experienced due to a car accident you had. But if you didn't take care of your car, leaving it with bald, flat tires, and a tire popped because of this mistake, that's your fault! You should have changed the tires. Or maybe you're sick and you don't take care of your body, so it gets worse. There are consequences for our actions. The Christian life does not make us immune to bad decisions; it invites us to follow the Good Shepherd, who knows exactly the way we should go. If you follow Him, He won't lead you astray. But He also won't hide you from the trials. King David didn't say that God would never let him go through the valley of the shadow of death, but that God would be *with him* in that valley.

> "The Christian life does not make us immune to bad decisions; it invites us to follow the Good Shepherd."

Even when you are making the right decisions, you will still have trials. Whether you are in full-time ministry, business, school, or whatever else, you will encounter them. It's how you look at the trials, and what (or who) you choose to be your source of comfort, that makes the difference. Many people allow damaging things into their lives to comfort them through trials. Cigarettes, alcohol, and many other things can become "comforters" in the suffering. But the next day, the pain is back, just worse. There's only one who can truly comfort you in your pain, and the side effects of His work are always good—Jesus.

So let's return to the question this chapter asks: What is the purpose of suffering? I think one thing needs to be established first. We are never going to fully

"It's how you look at the trials, and what (or who) you choose to be your source of comfort, that makes the difference."

understand everything that happens on this earth. Deuteronomy 29:29 says, "The secret things belong to the Lord our God, but those things which are revealed belong to us and to our children forever, that we may do all the words of this law." People try to figure it all out. They ask, "Why, why, why did this happen? Why did this tragedy happen? Why didn't I get the breakthrough I was hoping for?" Many times, people allow these questions to overwhelm them and drive them to despair. They never move on because they are held captive by these questions.

Some of the most successful colleges in America were founded on Christianity but are now the most atheistic schools. There are probably many reasons why this happened, but I think it might be partly because they went so deep to try and figure everything out that they got lost in the midst of it. It's not bad to ask questions, but we shouldn't get stuck if we don't receive an answer.

I won't go chasing after God asking *why* when He has not revealed the answer to me. Instead, I'm going to move on with my life and understand that God will work it for good in the end. If I keep meditating on the unknown, I'm not going to be productive with my life. But if I move forward and allow God to complete His good work, that's exactly what's going to happen. Keep moving forward, allow God to comfort you, abide in Him, and stand on His promises. We're not going to fully understand until we reach heaven, so before we get there, we need to learn to trust.

Whatever the source of our suffering is, God is able to use it for His purposes. Whether it is an attack from the enemy, the result of our bad choices, or even tests that God Himself allows us to have, there is a lot to gain through it all. He is kind and will not let these circumstances go to waste, if we will let Him do His work in us. If you want to have joy in suffering, you need to understand how God wants to change you through it all. Remember, He is your Father. He's not trying to destroy you. He loves you and wants the very best for you, because you are His child.

THE FATHER'S DISCIPLINE

Hebrews 12 is a great place to start if we want to discover God's purposes in our suffering. The first thing it shows us is that the Father will sometimes discipline us. Discipline often seems negative, but really, it's a beautiful thing. Every earthly parent disciplines his or her children for their good, so how much more will God discipline us for our good?

"My son, do not make light of the Lord's discipline, and do not lose heart when he rebukes you, because the Lord disciplines the one he loves, and he chastens everyone he accepts as his son."

HEBREWS 12:5–6 (NIV)

This passage in Hebrews is actually quoting from Proverbs 3:11–12. King Solomon wrote a lot about discipline in Proverbs. Here are some examples (from the NIV): "For lack of discipline they will die, led astray by their own great folly" (5:23); "Whoever heeds discipline shows the way to life, but whoever ignores correction leads others astray" (10:17); "Whoever loves discipline loves knowledge, but whoever hates correction is stupid" (12:1); "Discipline your children, and they will give you peace; they will bring you the delights you desire" (29:17). Do you see how important discipline is to God? It will keep you alive, cause you to walk in the *way of life,* give you knowledge, bring peace and delight, and so much more.

When I was a child, I decided to put my hand on a hot stove and, not surprisingly, badly burned it. I was told not to touch the stove, but I didn't listen, and now I have a scar on my hand because of my disobedience. This simple experience of suffering has disciplined me, so that I don't make the same mistake again. The same is true of God. Often He allows us to experience the consequences of our actions so that we don't continue making the wrong choices.

The one thing I held on to during my time in India was that God would turn everything for my good in the end. I knew this was true because I know that He is a good Father. As I said before, not all suffering is part of God's plan—sometimes it is because of our bad choices or the enemy trying to destroy us—so I don't believe that God gave me that sickness to discipline me. The reason I'm revisiting that story is because of the revelation that got me through the suffering: God is good.

You need to realize this truth when you experience the discipline of God: He only disciplines you because He *loves* you. He is a good Father who cares deeply for you, and He knows exactly what you need. He wants you to become more like Jesus, growing stronger in your faith every day. And He is committed to do whatever it takes to accomplish this, all because of His great love for you, His child. It might hurt for a bit, but it will produce good fruit in your life.

It makes me think of some "spiritual children" I

am investing in, some who have only recently been saved. They still have things in their lives that need to be removed, and it's important that I am able to lovingly correct them in these areas. The truth often hurts, but it sets us free. Not everybody wants to receive correction, but I want to see these guys change and become more fruitful, because I love them. The only way you can reach the potential God has for you is to embrace His discipline.

Count your hardships as discipline. Whatever you face in your life, don't look at these situations as negative, but as a sign that you are a legitimate child of God.

"The only way you can reach the potential God has for you is to embrace his discipline."

"If you endure chastening, God deals with you as with sons; for what son is there whom a father does not chasten? But if you are without chastening, of which all have become partakers, then you are illegitimate and not sons."

HEBREWS 12:7-8

When you experience discipline from God, it is proof that you are a legitimate son or daughter. This Scripture says that if you don't receive discipline, you are not a true child of God. If you want to walk through suffering with your head held high and in the joy of the Lord, you have to recognize your adoption as a son or daughter of the King. If you have the wrong perspective of God, you will think that He doesn't care, or that He is punishing you because He is angry. But when you know you are a son or daughter and co-heir with Christ, you will realize what a privilege it is to be disciplined by God.

In the Kingdom, orphans don't know they have a Father, but sons do. When you have received the revelation of sonship and you go through trials, you know you can trust your Father through it all. But if you are an orphan and don't realize who your Father is, you won't trust Him. You'll give in and go back to your old ways, you'll get discouraged, and you may even abandon your faith. If you understand your sonship, you'll see that your Father is there with you even in the darkness. When you're a son, you don't lose Christ in the midst of it—He is with you in the storm. And as you begin to trust Him as your Father, you will find that in the hardships, you will gain an even greater revelation of sonship. The more you trust Him in suffering, the more you will see how good a Father He is to you.

The Father disciplines us because of His great love. But it's not just so that we don't make the same mistakes again. It's also to train us so that we become fruitful in the ministry to which He has called us.

TRAINING IN RIGHTEOUSNESS

> "Now no chastening seems to be joyful for the present, but painful; nevertheless, afterward it yields the peaceable fruit of righteousness to those who have been trained by it."
>
> HEBREWS 12:11

When you go to the gym, you have to push your body if you want to see results. It's not until you stretch your muscles in pain that they actually start to grow. The same is true in our spiritual lives. God wants us to be strong in the Spirit, but we need to push through the trials of life in order to strengthen our spiritual muscles. You must be trained in both spiritual strength and understanding to be prepared for the missions ahead.

A father is not going to give his child the keys to his car if the child is only ten years old, no matter how

"God is training us and hardships are our discipline."

much the child pleads for them. There are some

things that we need to be prepared for before we can enter into them. The *harvest of righteousness* that Hebrews 12 talks about only comes to those who have been *properly trained*. God is training us, and hardships are our discipline. He will work it all out for our good in the end, but we must allow the hardships to do what they are designed to do. Many people do not have this understanding of suffering, so they run from their calling, purpose, or promotion once things get hard. But when we understand that suffering is used by God for our good, we can allow it to achieve its purpose in us and let Him mold and train us through it all—going from glory to glory.

The discipline might be painful, but if we will accept the training that it offers, we will see it produce the *peaceable fruit of righteousness* in our lives. Only those who have been trained bear this fruit. At school, you have to sit tests to prove that you have learned the curriculum. If you fail, you will probably have to sit the test again. In life, it's possible to go through the same trials and keep going through them until you have proven that you have learned what you need to.

Look at what happened to the Israelites after they left slavery in Egypt. God led them through the Red Sea and into the wilderness for a season. They were not supposed to be in the wilderness for as long as they were (forty years), but they were stuck there because of their complaining and murmuring. A whole generation never entered the Promised Land because they did not pass the test that God placed before them. Many people today go through suffering that is meant to bring about an increase in their lives, but because they don't receive the training on offer, they fail to enter the blessings of the Promised Land, whether it is because of complaining, doubting, or other things.

"The discipline might be painful, but if we will accept the training that it offers, we will see it produce the peaceable fruit of righteousness in our lives."

We need to understand this so that we can be as fruitful as possible in our lives. The Bible says, "My people are destroyed for lack of knowledge."[3] The lack of knowledge keeps us from the Promised Land. It kept the Israelites in the bondage of slavery even though they weren't slaves in Egypt anymore. Instead, they were slaves to endlessly wandering the wilderness. If you understand what God wants to do through your trials, you will have success.

Let me explain it like this. Right where you are now, if you close your eyes and you still know where everything around you is positioned without actually seeing it, you know you have been trained. You might even be able to successfully walk around your home in the dark without any problem. But if I place you in a dark room you have never seen, you will not know where anything is, and you'll bump into things as you try to move around—you will not have been trained.

"It yields a peaceable fruit to those that have been trained."[4] Fruit is yielded to the ones who have been

"The lack of knowledge keeps us from the promised land."

trained and have the right understanding. If you *are* trained, you don't need the lights, and you will progress through things more quickly. When we are properly trained by God, we can walk the right way even in the darkness. This book is to help train you to be aware of the joy of suffering so you can come out of your season better than you entered.

Many times when we go through hardships, things start to surface that we never knew were there. Perhaps it is bitterness, jealousy, unforgiveness, offense, lust, or certain desires we weren't aware of. What happens when you squeeze a lemon? Lemon juice comes out. What if orange juice comes out? Then it's not a lemon! It may be yellow—I've seen oranges that are yellow-colored—but it's still not a lemon. There are also some grapefruits that look like oranges, but if you cut one of them open and drink the juice, you will realize how sour it is. You don't realize it's a grapefruit until you open it.

The same is true when we face hardships. Suddenly we react in a certain way and realize that there was something impure in our hearts all along, but it had been hidden. God is so merciful that He uses suffering to expose these things in our hearts, not because He wants to shame us, but because He loves us and wants us to be free.

The Bible says that God withdrew His presence from King Hezekiah so he would know what was in his heart[5]—not for God to know, because He knows everything anyway, but for the king to see. One of the worst things I can imagine would be for God to remove His presence from me. I don't know what I would do without the sense of His presence. But this is exactly what happened to King Hezekiah. Maybe your hardship or suffering today is God removing His presence. Cheer up, friend, and realize God is with you and is working everything for your good; stick with what the Word of God says. At the end of the day, God is preparing us for heaven—as well as for our tasks on the earth.

God has a destination planned for us, but certain things might be slowing us down. If we allow God to operate and remove these things, *then* we can go where He wants us to go. If we are like the Israelites, struggling with the same sin over and over again, we won't go anywhere. It's important to allow God to surface certain things so that they can be removed. This process may take some time, so we have to trust that God knows what He is doing.

The process seems hard because we're such an instant generation—we want everything quickly. But we need to allow God to work things through in His own time. When you sharpen an axe, you might not see the difference right away. But after a time of sharpening each side continuously, you will notice how sharp it has become. As long as you are abiding in Jesus, you *will* bear fruit in due season. So long as we abide during the suffering, there will be fruit produced in our lives. Many times people try to produce their own fruit, and when they don't see the results immediately, they become discouraged. Instead, we need to allow God to produce the fruit of *His* Spirit in our lives.

I remember one time after I had just been saved, I dropped my phone and was so angry. The screen cracked, and I was upset for the rest of the day. Something so small and pathetic was able to ruin my entire day. A year or two later, I dropped my phone again. This time my response was, *That's cool, it's OK; I'll fix it later.* It was not a burden anymore. I remember sitting there, looking at the phone, and thinking, *Wow! Would you look at that! Usually I would be upset, but now it doesn't bother me.* We may not be able to discern it right away, but in due time—often when another test comes our way—we will see the process God has taken us through, and then we will have true joy.

Sometimes people will comment on the change God has performed in your life, but other times you will just see the change yourself. Perhaps you are reading the Word and you begin crying as the Holy Spirit wells up inside you with the compassion of God. And then you realize that you never had that compassion in you, but it is the result of God's work in your life up until that moment. It's easy to look back on the trials and thank God for the way they shaped us. But we should also choose to have joy in the midst of the trial, knowing that the end result will be blessing.

SHAKING THE NEST

I remember reading about how young eagles are trained by their mothers. The Bible also talks a little about eagles. These amazing birds seem to fly effortlessly, rising with the wind thermals, and can see a rabbit on the ground from three miles away! God promises that if we wait upon Him, we "shall mount up with wings like eagles."[6] You might want to be an "eagle" in the Kingdom, but first you will have to go through the right training to prepare you. What does this training look like?

A baby eagle is kept safe within its nest, away from predators that want to harm it, and is protected and provided for by its mother. But the safety of the nest is not going to last forever. Eventually, the young eagle will need to learn to fly, hunt, and care for itself and eventually its children. If it doesn't learn these things, it will never be able to survive once its mother has gone.

The same is often true in our lives. We are born again into God's family, and we may have people around us who can care for us, provide the spiritual nourishment we need, and keep us safe from the enemy through their intercession for us. And God Himself may provide us with a lot of safety as we begin our journey with Him. But He doesn't want us to stay as immature children. Eventually we need to move from milk to solid food.[7]

Hebrews 5:12–14 says, "For though by this time you ought to be teachers, you need someone to teach you again the first principles of the oracles of God; and you have come to need milk and not solid food. For everyone who partakes only of milk is unskilled in the word of righteousness, for he is a babe. But solid food belongs to those who are of full age, that is, those who by reason of use have their senses exercised to discern both good and evil." God wants you not just to be discipled, but to disciple others. And to do this, He must teach you how to fly.

When the time has come, something quite amazing happens! The mother eagle will shake the nest until its child falls out and begins plunging toward the ground. The first few times, the child might not be able to fly at all, so its mother will swoop down and catch it before it hits the ground. Eventually, after many attempts, the young eagle will learn to fly and will no longer need the mother's assistance.

If you are going through hardships, maybe God is trying to shake you out of your nest. It might seem scary at first, and you might feel like you are just falling to your death, but God will continue to pick you up again and again while you learn to strengthen yourself. The suffering might be exactly what you need to shake you out of your comfort zone and into the plans and purposes of God for your life. You might have prayed to be used by God, just like I did, and this is the way He can get you ready.

"The suffering might be exactly what you need to shake you out of your comfort zone and into the plans and purposes of God for your life."

Then when you face the storms of life, you can do just what the eagle does—rise with the wind and soar above the storm. Eagles are very good at predicting storms, so they know when they need to take flight. They don't try to flap violently to rise higher; they wait for the hot wind to come. The same is true for us. In our suffering and trials, we won't have any success if we try to defeat them in our strength. But God promises in Isaiah 40:31 that "those who wait on the Lord shall renew their strength; they shall mount up with wings like eagles, they shall run and not be weary, they shall walk and not faint." The wind of the Holy Spirit will carry you higher until you are flying above the storm, able to see from God's perspective.

Wouldn't it be better if God removed all suffering from the world? It might seem like it, but then we would miss out on so much that He has for us. If you can see His purpose, you will start to experience the joy of the Holy Spirit in ways you may never have before. Embrace the suffering as a greatly loved child of God. Draw near to Him, and watch as He draws nearer to you.[8]

3

REFINED BY FIRE

I THOUGHT my trials in India had come to an end, but they hadn't. There were more to come. The first time I travelled there, God showed me that I would return. Two years later, He sent me back for two-and-a-half weeks to preach the Gospel in a number of locations. But the very first day, I got sick with food poisoning. I was throwing up most of the night, and the next day, I had to drive three hours early in the morning to preach at a crusade in a different town. At that moment, I had a choice to make. I could give in to the discouragement, or I could believe the Word of God.

For a while before this moment, the Lord had been telling me to be strong and courageous, through many different circumstances and people. On one occasion, my little brother gave me surfing sunglasses out of the blue, and as I took them off one day, I noticed the words "Be strong and courageous" written on the side. A few months before I returned to India, I was in Mexico for a conference. After the service, I was in a room with some friends telling them how the Lord kept giving me this verse. All of a sudden, my phone vibrated with a message from my sister-in-law, saying, "Be strong and courageous." On the second night of this trip to India, while I was vomiting, the Lord said to me, "Stand on the Word." Not long after, I received a text message from my youth pastor with the same verse: "Be strong and courageous."[1]

The Bible calls the Lord the "God who gives endurance and encouragement."[2] To encourage is to *give courage.* When God speaks, they aren't just words. His words come with power. One man of God often says, "No freshly spoken word of God will ever come to you that does not contain its own ability to perform itself."[3] Whenever God speaks, you have an opportunity to receive power through His words. Each time He told me to be strong and courageous, He was offering me the power of His strength and courage to get through the trial I was facing. He will do the same for you, if you listen attentively to His voice.

Many people had discouraged me from going back to India because of what happened the first time.

I knew in the depths of my heart that I had to go. It turned out to be one of the most fruitful missions trips I have been on, yet it was the hardest. The first time it was dengue fever; this time I was in the hospital with heatstroke and food poisoning. To make matters worse, the main doctor said that his wife had recently died from the same thing.

It would have been easy to give in to the fear and disappointment, but I knew I had been sent there for a reason, and I was determined to see it through. I kept to my schedule, which meant that I would go outside and preach in the relentless Indian heat, see many people get saved, and quickly return to the air-conditioned car. Severely dehydrated, I would have to drink lots of fluids before I went back to preaching. It was exhausting and extremely difficult, but God was still moving through it all.

After a week's stay, I couldn't contact anyone because I had no internet on my phone. The pastor I was staying with shut off my Wi-Fi, and the trip organizer did not give me any data on my phone. He told me I shouldn't travel anywhere and even called around ten pastors and bishops over, who sat me down and told me I could not travel.

It was as if they held me hostage. They said I needed to stay with them and preach at their events. (Since the white man could gather a crowd, they wanted me to preach.) One pastor showed me videos (out of selfish motives) of people getting shot by gunmen in the place where I was planning to travel next. Fear filled me, and I was tempted to give in and stay back. But I refused and pressed on with my schedule.

Fortunately, I have some slow service with my USA phone company in many different countries, and when I put my SIM card in, I managed to get service and send my location to a friend who was a pastor. He then sent me a driver who brought me to the next location where I was headed.

When I arrived, no one was getting shot. It was just a fear tactic to control and use me. I had peace knowing the enemy tried to stop me from being in the next town because God had a great plan for me there —many people heard the Gospel and gave their lives to Jesus. No suffering or opposition could take away the joy of seeing the Kingdom of God expand in this world.

"No suffering or opposition could take away the joy of seeing the Kingdom of God expand in this world."

I had walked into the furnace and survived. But not only survived; I came back from that trip walking in new authority, and new doors began to open. That's what happens when we are refined by fire. We often pray for the fire of God—Jesus promised to baptize us with the Holy Spirit and fire—because we know that only this baptism will lead us into a supernatural lifestyle.

But fire burns. If you want to see the power of God released through your life, you have to yield to what God is doing in you. It might be uncomfortable at first, but it will produce good fruit if you abide.

THE SILVERSMITH & THE POTTER

"He will sit as a refiner and a purifier of silver."

MALACHI 3:3

The Bible talks about God as a refiner of gold and silver. The process of refining silver teaches us exactly what He means by this. A silversmith will start a fire and wait until it gets incredibly hot, then hold the silver over the fire until it is properly refined. The fire burns all of the impurities away so that what's left is pure silver. If the silver is left over the fire too long, it will be ruined, so the silversmith has to know the right time to remove it.

We don't always understand God's timing, but we need to trust that His wisdom is perfect. The fire is for purification, and if He pulled us out too early, we would still have impurities clinging to us. Remember this when it feels like your trial is never going to end. He wants you to be pure and holy, and His love is what keeps you in the fire. He promises that He "will not allow you to be tempted beyond what you are able, but with the temptation will also make the way of escape, that you may be able to bear it."[4]

The silversmith knows the refining is complete when he sees the image of himself as a reflection on the surface of the silver—when it's so shiny he can see his own face like in a mirror. God will allow us to stay in the fire until that perfect time when He can see Himself in us. We were all made in the image of God, designed to reflect Him to the world around us. But sin has corrupted us and destroyed that image. God's plan all along was to restore us to Himself so that once again we could be His reflection to the world. If you want people to see Jesus when they look at you, you have to embrace the refiner's fire.

Not only does the fire purify gold and silver, but it also allows it to be reshaped into whatever its maker desires. In order to create jewelry, something like a necklace or bracelet, you have to melt the metal. When it's melted, you can pour it into a mold that is shaped however you like. A similar example the Bible gives us is the potter and the clay—He is the Potter, we are the clay.

"Not only does the fire purify gold and silver, it also allows it to be reshaped into whatever its maker desires."

God knows what He wants to make out of you, and He will use the circumstances of life to accomplish it—so don't complain to the Potter about what He's doing. He is the Potter. He knows what He's doing, so let Him do His thing. God will shape and mold us because He knows what He's making out of us. Sometimes the potter even has to break the pottery down to remake it again.

I wanted to be used by God, but He needed to prepare me. The Bible says, "Therefore, if anyone cleanses himself from [what is dishonorable], he will be a vessel for honor, sanctified, useful to the Master, prepared for every good work."[5] If you are facing a test right now, let it remind you that God wants to transform you into an honorable vessel prepared for *every good work.*

You are like gold, silver, or clay in the hands of a loving God. He wouldn't allow you to go through the fire for no reason, only because the fire will refine

"If you are facing a test right now, let it remind you that God wants to transform you into an honorable vessel for every good work."

you and make you more beautiful and useful than ever. The process might feel strange, but if you are following Jesus, you shouldn't be surprised when it comes.

> "Beloved, do not think it strange concerning the fiery trial which is to try you, as though some strange thing happened to you; but rejoice to the extent that you partake of Christ's sufferings, that when His glory is revealed, you may also be glad with exceeding joy."
>
> 1 PETER 4:12–13

We often try to avoid the fire because we can't see the end result, and because we are so comfortable in our lives. Many of us who live in America have grown up with a lot of comfort compared to people in many other parts of the world. But if you read through the Book of Acts, you will see that the first Christians didn't enjoy the same lifestyle as us. They were persecuted, and many of them had to leave their cities and move to new places.

If you really want to be used by God, you have to be willing to leave the comfort zone. Before I travelled to India on my first missions trip, I was lukewarm in my faith. I went along to church and did the "Christian" things, but I wanted to enjoy the pleasures of the world. How many Christians are really on fire for Jesus, ready to lay their lives down for Him? How many churches are burning with a passion to win the lost and see revival in our nation?

In Revelation 3, Jesus spoke to the lukewarm believers of the Laodicean church. They thought they had everything they needed—money, influence, comfort—but Jesus had a different perspective. He said to them, "Because you are lukewarm, and neither cold nor hot, I will vomit you out of My mouth."[6] This is a pretty serious thing!

The solution is this: "I counsel you to buy from Me gold refined in the fire, that you may be rich; and white garments, that you may be clothed, that the shame of your nakedness may not be revealed; and anoint your eyes with eye salve, that you may see. As many as I love, I rebuke and chasten. Therefore be zealous and repent."[7]

If you are lukewarm in your faith, the refining fire is just what you need. And see what else Jesus says in this passage: "As many as I love, I rebuke and chasten." He says the same thing we read in Hebrews 12: "For whom the Lord loves He chastens."[8] He doesn't condemn you or shame you; instead, He invites you into the refiner's fire because He loves you.

THE FIERY FURNACE

You might feel like you are going into the fire at the moment. But there were three young men who were *literally* thrown into a fire. Shadrach, Meshach, and Abednego were in captivity in Babylon. God gave them great wisdom, which King Nebuchadnezzar noticed, and they were given great authority over the people of Babylon. They were young, talented, and lovers of God. But there came a time when all this would be tested.

The king set up a golden statue and commanded the people to bow down and

"For whom the Lord loves He chastens."

worship it whenever they heard the sound of the music. The punishment for disobeying the king was to be thrown into a burning fiery furnace. Even though the punishment was death, Shadrach, Meshach, and Abednego would not turn away from God and worship the king's statue, and so the king ordered for them to be thrown into the furnace. But they were ready for it. They knew that God would be with them, and yet they were content even without knowing if they would be saved.

Are you content going into the fire? Many of us want blessings but don't want to go into the furnace. These three young men went into the fire with courage. They said to the king, "Our God whom we serve is able to deliver us from the burning fiery furnace... But if not, let it be known to you, O king, that we do not serve your gods, nor will we worship the gold image which you have set up."[9]

The guards turned the heat in the furnace up seven times hotter than usual. Maybe the fire you are going through seems so much worse than what everyone around you is going through. Even so, God is preparing you for a miracle.

Shadrach, Meshach, and Abednego were bound with ropes and thrown into the fire. What happened next was supernatural.

First, the ropes on their hands burned. The very things that were holding them captive, that bound them, were broken because of the fire—just like when Paul and Silas worshipped God in prison and their chains fell off. The chains that bind you will be broken in the fire.

> "God fights for you and causes your enemies to be a footstool for you."

Second, the men that threw them into the fire were killed by the intensity of the fire. God fights for you and causes your enemies to be a footstool for you. The three young men were the ones thrown into the fire, but it was their enemies who died. Something similar happened in the story of Esther. Haman built gallows to hang Mordecai, Esther's cousin, because of his own jealousy and hatred for the Jews. But at the end of the day, Esther revealed Haman's plan to annihilate the Jews to King Xerxes, who ordered Haman to be hanged on the very gallows that he had built to kill Mordecai. The enemy might be scheming to destroy you, but if you abide in Jesus, you will see his plans defeated. There is nothing that the enemy will try to use against you that God will not work out for the good. The Word says that the enemy digs a pit for you, but he is the one who falls into it.[10]

As Shadrach, Meshach, and Abednego were in the fiery furnace, the king looked and saw four men walking in the midst of the

> "The enemy might be scheming to destroy you, but if you abide in Jesus, you will see his plans defeated."

fire. "They are not hurt," he said, "and the form of the fourth is like the Son of God."[11] As they yielded to the fire, Jesus was there with them, and they were unharmed. Just because you enter the fire does not mean God will not be in there with you. It changes everything when you know that God doesn't abandon you in your trials. It's in the fire that He is closer than ever.

When Shadrach, Meshach, and Abednego came out of the furnace, they didn't even have the smell of smoke on them, and none of their clothes were affected. They were promoted by the king, and God was glorified. Their suffering not only freed them from bondages, but it also brought revival to the region. King Nebuchadnezzar glorified God and proclaimed His power to the entire nation.

The fire produces purity, freedom from bondage, and revival around us. What an honor and joy to be used by God in such a way. These young men lived out 1 Peter 1:6–7, which says, "In this you greatly rejoice, though now for a little while, if need be, you have been grieved by various trials, that the genuineness of your faith, being much more precious than gold that perishes, though it is tested by fire, may be found to praise, honor, and glory at the revelation of Jesus Christ." They were found to have genuine faith, faith that was tested (literally) by fire, and the end result was God being glorified through the revelation of Jesus—the fourth man in the fire.

The fire of hardship will prove that your faith is genuine. If you really understand this, you can have joy in the midst of suffering. The Bible talks a lot about rejoicing in suffering. One example is when James tells us to "count it all joy when you fall into various trials" and specifically says that these trials are for the "testing of your faith."[12] When you stand up for your faith in the midst of a trial, others will see and desire what you have. God will be glorified through the fire and after the fire. It's not just in the aftermath, it's also in the midst of the suffering that He is glorified.

It's also important to have good friends around you in the fire. Shadrach, Meshach, and Abednego linked up and encouraged each other. Today it's normal for friends to drink, party, and watch and do impure things together. You need to find brothers and sisters who will go into the fire with you, uncompromising and free from the influences of the world. It's the mercy of God that He gives us brotherhood in the fire when His Son Jesus had to suffer alone.

Not only do we have fellowship with brothers and sisters who are with us, but we know that we are also united with people all over the world—fellow members of the body of Christ—who are experiencing the same kind of suffering we are. The Word tells us to "resist [the enemy], steadfast in the faith, knowing that the same sufferings are experienced by your brotherhood in the world."[13] God is raising up an army of believers all around the world who have been purified by fire so that they can bring revival to the ends of the earth.

In order for God to protect you in the fire, you must trust Him in the fire. You can't go in thinking that you can survive in your own strength. You must rely on His power to keep you steadfast. Don't be naive and think that you are invincible because of *your* great faith. That's one sure way to build yourself up with pride and put yourself in danger of a great fall. Instead, choose

"God is raising up an army of believers all around the world who have been purified by fire, so that they can bring revival to the ends of the earth."

humble confidence that God will be with you and *He* will strengthen you—then you will come out of the trial in power and purity.

> "When you pass through the waters, I will be with you; and through the rivers, they shall not overflow you. When you walk through the fire, you shall not be burned, nor shall the flame scorch you."
>
> ISAIAH 43:2

JOB

One of the most dramatic stories of suffering in the Bible is the story of Job. He was a blessed man— incredibly wealthy—and although we don't know much about the rest of his family, we know that Job was righteous before God. He would regularly wake up early in the morning to bring sacrifices and offerings on behalf of his family members, just in case they had sinned.[14]

Early on in the story, we see a conversation going on between God and Satan. Job (and his family and friends) knew nothing about this conversation at the time, but we get to see exactly what was going on. The Bible says that Satan had come "from going to and fro on the earth, and from walking back and forth on it."[15] And God said to Satan, "Have you considered My servant Job, that there is none like him on the earth, a blameless and upright man, one who fears God and shuns evil?"[16] Satan was going throughout the earth, and God recommended Job to him.

The enemy is still going around today seeking those who walk righteously and blamelessly before God—people who turn away from evil. God Himself offered up Job to the enemy that he might test him and take him through a time of suffering. The Book of Job shows us why we suffer. It shows us how Job was tested.

Everything was taken from Job except his life—the one thing God would not give Satan permission to take. God wanted to demonstrate that there was a man who loved Him not for what he could get from God, but simply for who He is. Even after losing everything, Job would still stand faithful to God. Have you ever thought about this when you were going through hardships? Do you love God for the things He gives to you, or simply for who He is? Sometimes the trials will reveal where our hearts are—whether good or bad.

Notice the very first thing Job does after everything is taken away from him: "Then Job arose, tore his robe, and

"Do you love God for the things He gives to you, or simply for who He is?"

shaved his head; and he fell to the ground and worshiped."[17] Would we do the same? Is our default to worship God no matter what our circumstances? The Bible then says, "In all this Job did not sin nor charge God with wrong."[18] Maybe in your mind you have been accusing God of wrongdoing. Take the opportunity to repent of this mindset and turn your heart back to Him in worship.

Job had three friends who came to visit him after all of this had happened. All three of these friends fought against Job by applying their *theology* to the things that they saw. They tried to tell Job that God wouldn't allow these hardships to come to someone who was righteous; therefore, he must have some kind of sin in his life. But Job had brought himself before God and repented of everything he could think of, and he still couldn't understand why he was going through all of this. Job didn't worship God because he understood it all; he worshipped God because He is

God. Don't make the mistake of waiting until you have all the answers before you worship.

"Job didn't worship God because he understood it all; he worshipped God because he is God."

Many times people try to create their own theology to explain why people suffer. Sometimes we do the same as we try to understand everything. It was a confusing situation for Job and his friends. It seemed like Job must have done something wrong, but we can see what was really going on: God was offering up Job as a righteous servant so that he might be proven faithful, even through the most intense fire. What seemed to be turmoil, chaos, suffering, and potentially punishment for sin was actually proving that Job was a righteous man. It was proving that he could go through these trials and stay faithful. He was chosen out of all the people on the earth! What seemed bad was actually good—he had been chosen as God's vessel and walked through it all with a faithful heart.

In the end, God blessed Job with double the possessions he had lost. There are things that happen in the background that we often do not see. God is a just God, He's a fair God, and He's in control. We might not understand why everything happens the way it does—it's not always for us to understand—but we must always trust God while we walk through. We must trust Him through these trials, tribulations, and sufferings, knowing that He is faithful to the end.

Job knew what it was like to go through the refiner's fire. He said, "But [God] knows the way that I take; when He has tested me, I shall come forth as gold."[19] He knew that just like gold or silver is placed into a blazing hot fire to purify it, so he would be purified in the fire that God had allowed him to experience. We should have the same confidence as Job, knowing that in the end, we will come out of the fire like refined gold, ready for the next chapter of our calling.

4

THE SUFFERINGS OF CHRIST

SUFFERING IS RARELY a sign of failure. It often comes before great success. Nowhere is this clearer than in the life of Jesus. We know that the Son of God was perfect and sinless in everything He did and said; never once did He stray from His Father's will or give in to the temptations of the enemy. He was fully obedient, totally pure and holy, and the Father was "well pleased" with Him.[1]

But still, Jesus suffered, and His sufferings were more than any of us could imagine. If you look in your Bible at Isaiah 53, you might see "The Suffering Servant" or something similar as the chapter heading. Hundreds

> "Suffering is rarely a sign of failure. It often comes before great success. Nowhere is this clearer than in the life of Jesus."

of years before Jesus was born, the Father had already spoken that His Son would be known for His sufferings. We love this chapter of the Bible because it promises forgiveness, healing, and peace for us all. But sometimes we forget what Jesus had to go through to accomplish all of this for us. If you read through Isaiah 53, you will see many examples of His suffering:

- **Verse 3:** He was despised and rejected by men. He was a man of sorrows. He was acquainted with grief.
- **Verse 4:** He bore our griefs. He carried our sorrows.
- **Verse 5:** He was wounded for our transgressions. He was bruised for our iniquities. He was punished so that we could have peace. He was whipped for our healing.
- **Verse 7:** He was oppressed and afflicted. He was led like a lamb to slaughter.
- **Verse 8:** He was cut off from the land of the living.
- **Verse 9:** He was buried with the wicked.

That's not a list of experiences you or I would enjoy going through. We would probably run away from all of them. But Jesus came to die. He came to shed His blood and to give His life as a ransom for us.

He endured the cross and was made a curse for us. They put Him through the worst and most humiliating death a man could die. The soldiers beat Him so badly that He couldn't even be recognized. And apart from all the physical suffering, His own people denied and rejected Him. None of us has suffered like Jesus did.

Even from a young age, Jesus had to deal with a world that didn't understand Him. He had to be incredibly patient and wait for thirty years before His ministry could begin. When He was

"Hundreds of years before Jesus was born, the Father had already spoken that His Son would be known for His sufferings."

just twelve years old, His parents left Him in the temple without realizing it, only to find Jesus listening to the teachers and asking them questions. The people around Him were amazed at the understanding of such a young boy, but His parents didn't fully understand His calling.[2] When God calls us, we want to tell everybody about it. But sometimes even the people closest to you won't fully understand. If that's you, just remember that Jesus experienced the same thing. The Bible even says about Jesus, "Though

He was a Son, yet He learned obedience by the things which He suffered."[3]

As Jesus began His ministry, the religious leaders —Scribes and Pharisees—constantly opposed Him and looked down upon Him. "Oh, he's just a carpenter," they might have said. "He's just a young kid. He doesn't know anything. We're the Pharisees, the Scribes, and the religious leaders." Jesus was accused of being demon-possessed,[4] attacked for spending time with sinners,[5] and several times, the people tried to kill Him before His ministry was complete. After His relative and the man God had sent to prepare the way for Him, John the Baptist, was beheaded, Jesus tried to get away and spend some time alone, but the crowds followed Him. Even though He must have been grieving, He still had compassion on the people and healed the sick.[6]

> "Even though He must have been grieving, He still had compassion on the people and healed the sick."

But even through all of this, Jesus was never insecure about His calling. He never felt the need to fight back, argue, or dominate others. He simply listened to His Father and was obedient to everything He heard and saw. Maybe God has called you, and the people around you, even family and friends, don't understand your calling. Most people think that life is all about getting a good-paying job and looking after your family. So what happens when God calls you to do something more radical and risky? Maybe you are being attacked by others for preaching the Gospel or standing up for the truth. Jesus' example is for you—don't fight back and try to argue your way to victory. Remember that Jesus has already secured your victory, and persevere in obedience to your calling. At the end of the day, if you are obedient, you will see great fruit in your life.

Before His death, Jesus was in the Garden of Gethsemane fighting through the pain and turmoil of His approaching crucifixion. It got so bad that He started sweating drops of blood because of the stress, because He knew the suffering He was about to face. He knew He would be mocked, spit on, cursed, beaten, and crucified. Jesus lived with the reality of His future suffering all throughout His life. And at the moment when He most needed His disciples, they were asleep, unable to stay up in prayer with Him. Think about it: Jesus Himself said, "Let this cup pass."[7] He was basically saying, "Let this pain pass." But then He turned it around and said to the Father, "Let your will be done."[8] He knew how bad the pain would be, but He also knew that He had to face it. Jesus was focused on the fruit of His suffering, not on the pain. As we focus on Jesus, He will help us to see the fruit and purpose and get through our season.

Jesus told His disciples several times that He was going to die. When Jesus was with them, they were passionate and all wanted to die for Him. Thomas said to his fellow disciples, "Let us also go, that we may die with Him."[9] But when it actually happened, they all failed. How many people lift their hands during worship, saying, "Jesus, I give You everything!" but when they leave, they give Him nothing? They say, "I give You my whole life, Lord," but once they leave the building, it's as if nothing ever happened. Many people deny Jesus through their disobedience.

Some of Jesus' closest friends betrayed Him. Peter denied that he even knew Jesus. All the disciples scattered, and Jesus was left alone. Judas sold Him out for thirty pieces of silver, yet Jesus still kept him around knowing full well that he would betray Him. Judas sold Jesus out with a kiss, which in those times was a sign of high respect. One of Jesus' closest companions stabbed Him in the back. Yet Judas pushed Jesus into His purpose. In your life, there will be Judas-like people that push you into your destiny and purpose, even though they betray you, even though they might push your buttons, even though they snitch you out and speak falsely about you.

The most painful moment for Jesus must have been when He cried out, "My God, My God, why have You forsaken Me?"[10] This must have been the hardest moment for Jesus to experience, for the first time in all of eternity, He was separated from the Father. As He took the sins of the world upon Himself, His Father had to turn away from the sight of His Son, who was now carrying the weight of our sins. Jesus had lived in perfect connection to the Father for eternity, but for the first time, He was cut off from the Father, experiencing the wrath of God. I can't imagine how much He suffered in that moment.

It was the will of Jesus to go through this suffering. He came to die for us. That is what got Him through —He focused on the end result. He would die on the cross, but then He would defeat death and make a way for us to get into heaven. We ate from a live tree and died; Jesus hung on a dead tree to bring us life. He flipped the switch. If the enemy knew what Jesus was doing, he would never have killed Him. The devil got shamed there.

As hard as everything was, it was the end result and the strength He obtained from the secret place with His Father that got Jesus through. The disciples may have denied and deserted Him at the most difficult time, but after Jesus had been resurrected and the disciples were filled with the Holy Spirit, they became truly ready to die for Him—and most of them *did* die brutal deaths for His sake.

Jesus went through the most intense pain and

suffering. He endured the cross and the shame that was connected with it, dying the worst kind of death possible. Not only did He go through the pain in the moment of His crucifixion, but He went through it in His spirit beforehand, knowing all that was going to be done to Him. He was truly the "Suffering Servant" who endured the worst pain so that you and I could be reconciled to the Father.

LOOKING UNTO JESUS

What would it have been like to suffer so intensely like Jesus did? How did He manage to pull through? Of course, it was because of His great love for us that He chose the suffering, so that all who believe in Him could be reconciled to the Father. But Hebrews 12 gives us another reason why Jesus could endure it all: joy.

> "Therefore we also, since we are surrounded by so great a cloud of witnesses, let us lay aside every weight, and the sin which so easily ensnares us, and let us run with endurance the race that is set before us, looking unto Jesus, the author and finisher of our faith, who for the JOY that was set before Him endured the cross, despising the

shame, and has sat down at the right hand of the throne of God."

HEBREWS 12:1-2 (EMPHASIS ADDED)

Jesus is the perfect example for us to follow. He was able to face suffering because He was strengthened by joy. He could see what was ahead of Him—that the end result would far outweigh the pain. What got Him through was looking to the Father and gaining strength from Him. The way through your struggle is not only by having a revelation of the fruit you will see after the suffering, but also by looking to the Father and receiving His strength.

What was Jesus' end result? That we would be saved because of the price He paid on the cross. And how did He gain strength from His Father? He lived in constant intimacy and knew He was the beloved Son in whom God was well pleased, and surrendered fully to the Father's will.

"The way through your struggle is not only by having a revelation of the fruit you will see after the suffering, but also by looking to the Father and receiving His strength."

As we run our race, whether it feels like we are running uphill or downhill, we need to keep our eyes focused on Jesus and remember what He had to endure for us. Along with this, the Word of God says that we need to throw off every weight and sin that is slowing us down. We will need strength to endure the suffering; there is no point in having extra baggage to carry along the way.

"For consider Him who endured such hostility from sinners against Himself, lest you become weary and discouraged in your souls. You have not yet resisted to bloodshed, striving against sin."

HEBREWS 12:3-4

If you are feeling weary or discouraged, just remember. Remember the hatred, the mockery, the whipping, the crucifixion, and everything else. Be encouraged that because of the suffering of Christ, you don't have to pay the price for your own sin. You don't need to be whipped in order to receive your healing—Jesus has already done it. You don't need to carry your own sickness and pain—Jesus has already carried it for you. You don't need to be pierced and crushed to pay for your own sin—Jesus has already been pierced and crushed for you. You don't need to be punished for your sin—Jesus has already taken the punishment so that you can have peace with God.

Seeing the fruit of Jesus' suffering allows us to have hope in the midst of our trials. His fruit was our salvation, defeating the devil, taking the keys back, and so much more. Seeing His fruit helps us to trust Him to produce fruit in *our* lives. You will find strength to face your suffering if you look at the fruit of Jesus' life, look at His promises to you, and receive comfort and joy through intimacy with Him.

It's not up to you to have strength for the trial. In the Old Covenant, God was with His people, but the Holy Spirit had not been poured into them. Now, in the New Covenant, Jesus is living in you by the power and presence of the Holy Spirit. The disciples weren't ready for suffering under the Old Covenant, but when the Holy Spirit had come to dwell in them, they were empowered to face it like they couldn't before. Never face suffering without Jesus, but trust in the power of the Holy Spirit to strengthen you and give you joy. You need Jesus to help you to suffer; He causes it to be a joy. After the Holy Spirit came, the disciples were able to suffer with joy. Many times we read men like Paul, Peter, and James talk about the joy it is to partake in His sufferings.

But that joy is only possible through the Holy Spirit. Where the Spirit of the Lord is, there is freedom. Coming into His presence sets you free from your burdens. He invites you to take His yoke upon you—it's light. When we come to Him *for* Him, we will receive strength. (When we come to Him for something other than Him, we miss Him.) Abiding in Him is the most important thing. Once you get a glimpse of Him, He sets you free. There is joy in the suffering, because *He* is there.

LAZARUS

There was another moment of suffering in Jesus' life that I want to talk about, because it helps us see life from Jesus' perspective. During His ministry, Jesus spent a lot of time in a place called Bethany. While He was there, He often spent time in the home of Mary and Martha, who had a brother named Lazarus. We know that Mary loved Jesus greatly—she was the one who poured perfume on Him and wiped His feet with her hair. When these sisters sent word to Jesus about Lazarus' sickness, they said, "Lord, behold, he whom You love is sick."[11] Lazarus was a good friend of Jesus.

When Jesus found out that Lazarus was sick, He said, "This sickness is not unto death, but for the glory of God, that the Son of God may be glorified through it."[12] But instead of going straight to heal Lazarus, He waited two days before leaving for Bethany. During this delay, Lazarus died.

> "There is joy in the suffering, because He is there."

When Jesus finally arrived, Martha said to Him,

"Lord, if You had been here, my brother would not have died."[13] If anything is a suffering moment, this is it. There was a lot of mourning and sadness. My question is, why would Jesus wait two days? Lazarus would've been healed if He hadn't delayed.

Jesus reassured Martha by telling her that her brother would rise again. Martha said, "I know that he will rise again in the resurrection at the last day."[14] Martha only knew Jesus in a limited way. She didn't realize that His resurrection power could be seen now. While so much was going on outside the tomb of Lazarus, we read these words:

"Jesus wept."

JOHN 11:35

Why would Jesus weep? He had waited two days, even though He could have come earlier. He knew that He could raise Lazarus from the dead.

I believe that Jesus wept because the people lacked the revelation of who He was. They didn't know His nature fully. God is weeping for us to know Him more, and the suffering we experience allows us to discover more of His nature. The whole scene was full of doubt and disappointment in the midst of suffering, but then Jesus called Lazarus out of the grave, and he walked out even though he had been dead for four days!

The people had known Jesus as the Healer—He had healed many people up until this time—but now they knew Him as the Resurrector. The two days of pain they endured caused them to receive the revelation of Jesus as the resurrection and life. From that point on, they knew that He was not just the Healer, but also the Resurrector. Jesus wants to give us revelation through the Holy Spirit—revelation of who He is —through the suffering, if we will allow Him to do this. We might not understand what He is doing, but He knows. Allow Him to fulfill His work and take you deeper into the revelation of His nature. Oh, what a joy it is to have a deeper revelation of who He is!

UNION WITH JESUS

Jesus went through it all for us—for our salvation, for our freedom, to help us in our suffering; He endured it all. And now we can partake in suffering and become intimate with Him through it.

We become one with Him not just through intimacy in prayer, but also through intimacy in suffering. Sometimes we allow

> "We become one with Him not just through intimacy in prayer, but also through intimacy in suffering."

suffering to pull us away from God. Maybe it's because we blame Him for our pain, or we think we just have to deal with the struggle ourselves. But His heart has always been for us to draw near to Him in the midst of the suffering.

There's a union and intimacy with God that we find through prayer, worship, waiting on Him, and meditating on the Word. But there's also a different kind of intimacy that you will never experience unless it comes through suffering, just like the couple who has gone through thick and thin together, "for better, for worse, for richer, for poorer, in sickness and in health," like the wedding vows say. I'm not married, but I know the couples I've seen that are closer and more intimate in love are the ones who made it through battles together. They didn't just survive; they walked and talked together through it all. You need to walk and talk with Christ through the trial. We are not meant to just plow through it and come out stronger. No. There's something that Christ wants you to gain in this place. Take it. Receive it.

"But there's also a different kind of intimacy that you will never experience unless it comes through suffering."

Just like the subject of identity that we looked at earlier in the book, there are many revelations of the nature of Christ that you won't gain anywhere except for the storms of life. The people in Bethany only discovered the resurrection power of Jesus after Lazarus had been dead for four days. Through your suffering, you will see resurrection power, just like Lazarus did. You will gain a revelation that the people around Lazarus gained.

However, it's one thing to receive revelation about what Jesus can do, but another to truly become intimate with Jesus. Suffering is an invitation to partake in Christ through *His* sufferings. We become one with Him in the suffering. He knows what it's like to suffer, and it is when we humble ourselves, get on our knees, and cry out to Him that we become one with Him. Pursue intimacy—in-to-me-you-see. There's a seeing into Christ that you obtain through the suffering.

We plow through suffering no matter how we feel. But don't just plow through; receive from it. And

> "There's a seeing into Christ that you obtain through the suffering."

how much you will receive is up to you. Ask Him, "Lord, what can I gain from this? I don't want to just go through this for nothing. I want to gain something." Do you know what you're going to gain? Deeper intimacy. You understand Him, because He understands you.

If we are really hungry to know Jesus more, we will embrace whatever it takes to make that possible.

If it is suffering that will bring us closer to Him, we will be joyful knowing that it is forming us into the image of Christ. It pushes us closer to Him, which is a joyful thing for everyone who is hungry. Do we thank Him for these times? *Thank You, God, for loving me enough to not allow me to stay the same!* And if the suffering is what is going to change me, I'll thank Him for using it for my good.

Suffering and intimacy go together all throughout Scripture. Many of the prophets and patriarchs of old walked through intense suffering. But they were close to the heart of God. Paul said he wanted to know Christ, "the power of His resurrection, and the fellowship of His sufferings."[15] So often we want to know His power, but we stay away from His suffering. Another word for "fellowship" is "intimacy." Do you know the intimacy of Jesus' suffering?

The Word of God says, "For we do not have a High Priest who cannot sympathize with our weaknesses, but was in all points tempted as we are, yet without sin."[16] During His life on earth, Jesus was tempted, or tested, in every way that we are. And we know that because He experienced the tests and "suffered, being tempted, He is able to aid those who are tempted."[17]

We can never complain that God doesn't understand what we are going through, no matter how painful it is. When we realize the depths of the sufferings of Christ, we can see that He knows exactly what it feels like. We've talked about these tests we have in life and how important it is to take them seriously, so we have to retake them. Take the test and see what you can gain from it. See the union with Christ and His revelation that you can receive from the test. Otherwise you'll miss the treasure, because He works it all together for your good. If you're in sync with Him, you're going to receive the goodness He has to give to you.

Sometimes we are even tested in the blessing. It is easy to be complacent when things are going well, and we can forget to draw near to Jesus. But we need to always be in worship, whether times are good or bad. The Israelites came back to God again and again when times were hard, but in the prosperity, they forgot Him. If we learn to truly worship when times are good, the hardship will not overpower us, because we will simply continue to worship Him like we always have. That is the secret to facing suffering. Don't wait until it arrives to be intimate with Jesus. Start now, and then you will already be in the flow of the Spirit, and He will carry you through the trials.

The Bible says, "Blessed are the poor in spirit, for theirs is the kingdom of heaven. Blessed are those who mourn, for they shall be comforted."[18] God looks for a broken and contrite heart. This is the place where He waits for us, in the midst of the brokenness. When we least feel like He's there, that's where He is. The key is to press in to Him during those times and allow yourself to become one with Him. I've had many times where I just had to press in to God, and He became more real to me—not just in the good, but also in the bad. It was actually through the bad that He became the most real to me. He would speak, and I would know He was there, more clearly than at any other times.

There are things that come out in the struggles that don't come out anywhere else. There are certain characteristics that come out during times of chaos that don't come out anywhere else. And you will see a side of God in suffering that you may not see at any other time. You will see His comfort.

COMFORT OF THE HOLY SPIRIT

Before Jesus ascended into heaven, He promised His disciples that He would send "the Comforter."[19] He was not going to leave us alone to walk out this life, but always planned to send the Holy Spirit to live in us. The Holy Spirit is the Comforter. And you will get to experience His comfort when you find yourself in an *uncomfortable* situation.

It's never easy to go through the hardships of life,

but it's much easier when you have the Comforter walking with you as you are abiding in Him. When it's your burden to carry, it can weigh you down to the point of despair. But if you let Him carry it for you by dying to self daily, the burden will no longer be yours to bear. It will become a joy because He is with you through it all if you will allow Him to be, and because there is joy on the other side of the trial.

"The Holy Spirit is the comforter. And you will get to experience His comfort when you find yourself in an uncomfortable situation."

If you will welcome the Comforter, the Holy Spirit, into your life during times of hardship, you will find that He is glad to be with you. And along the way, you will hear Him whisper things like, "Fear not, for I am with you; be not dismayed, for I am your God. I will strengthen you, yes, I will help you, I will uphold you with My righteous right hand,"[20] and "[Cast] all your anxiety on him because he cares for you."[21]

5

THE AFTERMATH

IT'S easy to become discouraged when the walls of life seem to be crumbling around you and the promises of God appear to lie in ruins. I've been thinking a lot about the story of Nehemiah, someone who knew this reality well. He experienced his fair share of suffering, personally and together with his people, but he knew what it meant to persevere to the end.

The story starts with a report that the walls of Jerusalem were broken down and the gates burned with fire. Nehemiah wept when he heard this about the city he loved. Jerusalem, the city where God was meant to dwell, was in ruins.

At the time, Nehemiah was in captivity in Persia with many other Jews. The king gave him permission to return to Jerusalem to rebuild its walls. This was an exciting time for everyone as they looked forward to a restored and revived city. But as soon as they began this project, they faced intense opposition, especially from two men—Sanballat and Tobiah. Nehemiah says, "They laughed at us and despised us."[1] Later on, we are told, "[Sanballat] was furious and very indignant, and mocked the Jews."[2] These men went even further and conspired to attack Jerusalem with armies from the surrounding regions. They wanted to create confusion and stop the work, but Nehemiah and the people kept going. They believed in the vision so much that nothing was going to stop them.

When Sanballat and Tobiah heard that Nehemiah had finished rebuilding the wall, they suggested a meeting with him, planning to do him harm. Then they sent letters threatening Nehemiah, trying to scare him. They even sent a false prophet to try to put fear into him, but Nehemiah realized that this "prophet" wasn't sent from God.

The enemy wants to bring chaos to the people around you in order to try to stop the work. He will mock you and threaten you. His goal is to cause you to fall into sin so that he can use it against you. He wants you to fight fire with fire. And when your eyes aren't on God, you'll fall for the enemy's schemes—just like Peter, who started sinking as soon as he took his eyes off Jesus. This is why it's so important to have vision. If the people didn't know what the end goal was, they might have given up easily. But because they could see the aftermath, nothing could stop them. The same is true in your life. When the enemy tries to bring confusion and fear, just remember the promises God has given you.

Remember what Paul said to Timothy: "This charge I commit to you, son Timothy, according to the prophecies previously made concerning you, that by them you may wage the good warfare."[3] When you receive prophetic words from God, He is showing you what is to come so that when the enemy tries to sow seeds of doubt in your mind, you will be able to fight because you can see the aftermath.

Nehemiah kept building the wall because he knew that God was with him and would help him win the victory and finish this wall. He remained focused on the Lord. He knew that the wall would be finished even with all the hindrances and the hardships that were in the way to stop him. It's funny how it works— usually, when you face obstacles, it shows you are doing something right. Friend, do not give in and give up. This generation needs you. They need your reve- lation of the Father after this season.

After the wall was finished, revival broke out across the land for many years. During this time, the people would bring their offerings to the storehouse. However, later on, in

"This generation needs you, they need your revelation of the Father after this season."

chapter 13, we read that Nehemiah returned and found out that Tobiah had been living in the store-house, where the people's offerings were meant to go. (Remember, Tobiah was one of the guys who had taunted Nehemiah while he was building the wall.) Now that Tobiah was living there, because the corrupt priest had let him in, the people couldn't bring their offerings (worship), and the revival stopped. Something else was taking up the room, so the people could not bring their sacrifice and bring true worship.

When Tobiah began living in the storehouse, the priests and Levites left their callings—a percentage of the offerings would go to them to provide for their families, so without offerings coming in, they went back to working regular jobs. Some of us today have put "Tobiahs" in the place where worship is meant to be. We have allowed other things to reign in the place where worship should be. Maybe it's worry or fear; maybe it's sin; maybe it's greed or money; maybe it's lust or even pride from our achievements. Friend, remove the Tobiah and allow a fresh river to flow into your life. In times of hardship, those things will come out—if we have worship in there, we will automatically worship in the midst of struggles.

Even if you are in the midst of revival, that doesn't mean there won't still be trials and things that come in and try to steal your attention. The enemy will try anything to stop what God is doing. But Nehemiah was persistent through the attacks, suffering, hardship, and confusion, and he ended up succeeding.

Why did Nehemiah push through with building the walls even though he faced so much opposition? He knew how important the job was, and he could see the aftermath. He could see the revival that would come and the restoration of true worship to the city of Jerusalem. If God has called you to some task, make sure you ask Him to give you vision—"Where there is no vision, the people perish."[4] When you can see the aftermath—all the blessings that are ahead of you— nothing will be able to stop you from finishing the work God has called you to do.

So what can we expect after the suffering?

FRUITFULNESS

God has made it possible for us to experience joy while we are still suffering. But there will come a time when you finally see the breakthrough you have been praying for. Maybe it's the healing you need, a financial miracle, or the restoration of a relationship. Whatever your trial is, and no matter how long you have been going through it, there is always a moment of freedom when you step into the next season of life: the aftermath.

Paul said, "If in this life only we have hope in Christ, we are of all men the most pitiable."[5] He doesn't mean that we won't have blessings in this life, but that we need to always keep our eyes on heaven, where all suffering will cease. But God wants us to bear fruit in this season. In order for a seed to grow and bear fruit, it has to be planted—put in the dirt. Then it can grow to its full potential. And if it has been properly pruned, it will bear a lot of fruit.

"The more we allow God to prune us and cut off anything that doesn't need to be there, the more fruitful we will become for ourselves and others."

The fruit of your life will not just benefit you; it will also benefit those around you. An apple tree doesn't eat apples! It benefits those around it who eat of its fruit. The more we allow God to prune us and cut off anything that doesn't need to be there, the more fruitful we will become for ourselves and others.

There may be seasons when you are constantly investing into someone else and you feel discouraged because you don't see any fruit. There was a guy I invested a lot of time into—probably around two years. At the time, I didn't see any fruit. Eventually, he started a business, and then after a while, he became very fruitful. Everything that was sowed during those two years was sowed for that moment. Now I am made joyful by seeing the fruit in his life.

It's easy to be thankful when we look back on difficult seasons in our lives. We can see what God was doing to train and equip us, and how we are better now because of it. But it can be hard to be thankful while we are still in the trial. So we have to look to the aftermath and see what blessings await us on the other side. The Bible is full of promises that we will see breakthrough, no matter what trial we are going though.

"Weeping may endure for a night, but joy comes in the morning."

PSALM 30:5

"You have turned for me my mourning into dancing; You have put off my sackcloth and clothed me with gladness."

PSALM 30:11

"Those who sow in tears shall reap in joy."

PSALM 126:5

The only reason the enemy attacks us is because he knows there is something on the other side worth resisting. Just look at Jesus' fruit: He was raised from the dead! Because He suffered and died, and was then raised to life, His mission was multiplied throughout the earth. Everything Jesus did had a purpose; He never suffered for no reason. Ultimately, because of His suffering, He paid the price for the forgiveness of sins and opened the way for the Holy Spirit to come and fill His people. He was highly exalted by the Father and given the name above every other name.[6] Now Jesus is reaping His reward, which is all of us, and He is living inside us. We, the Church, are the reward given to Jesus. He suffered everything so that He could redeem us back to Himself as His bride. If Jesus' fruit doesn't excite you, nothing else will.

Look at Joseph, David, Daniel, and Moses. All these men walked through suffering but saw great fruit. Joseph went from a prison to the palace. David was a fugitive running away from King Saul, who was trying to kill him, but afterward, he also ended up in the palace. Daniel was put in charge after being thrown into the lions' den. In a moment, God took

93

these men from the pit to the palace. He can solve your problem overnight. When Moses was called to lead the people of Israel out of Egypt, he faced many difficulties and great opposition. But through it all, he saw incredible signs and wonders, like the Red Sea parting and supernatural provision of food in the wilderness.

In Joseph's case, he continued to honor God and serve others while he was in prison. His gifts still functioned in the struggle. You could easily get discouraged and just sit in the corner, but God wants to continue using you during the trial. David was used by God even before he became king. All of these men saw fruit in their suffering, but also great breakthrough and exaltation. If you are in the middle of a trial, remember that God wants you to bear good fruit both during and after. You can look forward to the day when you have passed the test and God has entrusted you with greater things.

The Book of Acts shows the fruit of the coming of the Holy Spirit. Through great persecution, the Gospel was spread throughout the world. Suffering pushes you into your calling and destiny. Many of us are afraid to step into our calling when it looks stormy. But the disciples went where Jesus called them, even when a storm was raging on the sea. As they did, Peter discovered a new revelation: that he could walk on water if he kept his eyes on Jesus.

Remember what Paul said: "For I consider that the sufferings of this present time are not worthy to be compared with the glory which shall be revealed in us."[7] God has prepared glory for you to walk in. If you really believe this, you can go through anything with joy in your heart. The present may be full of suffering, but the aftermath is glory.

AUTHORITY & INTIMACY

I always experienced an increase after suffering. When I returned from India, I started seeing miracles in the streets of America like I never had before. Many things God had spoken into my heart started happening in the aftermath of this trip.

On another occasion, I went on a trip to Mexico on my own. When I landed, I didn't know what was going to happen. I got into a car, and as we drove, all I could hear was the word "cartel" being said over and over again. I was afraid and was going through intense spiritual warfare. I knew God had called me, but in that moment, it was a struggle. I was brought to a house, and the pastor arrived in a brand-new truck to take me to the hotel. Everything turned out fine, and I preached the Word just as God had called me to.

When I came back from this trip, I knew I had stepped into a new level of authority in the Spirit. I started moving in more power, seeing more miracles, and new doors began to open. It seems like this is the process God takes me through every time. First He speaks to me and reveals what He wants to do through my life. Then He allows me to go through trials so that the word He has spoken can be tested. Finally, after the test, there is great fruitfulness. He who is tested can be trusted.

"He who is tested can be trusted." It wasn't just new authority that I saw. Through the suffering, I saw my identity in Christ more clearly than ever. Because of this, I didn't need the approval of men anymore; I simply needed to believe what God had spoken to me and be obedient to His calling. The disciple John described himself as the one whom Jesus loved. He knew who he was in Christ. Through the hardships I have faced, I now know that I have everything in Christ.

Everything I went through made me the person I am today. I have found Christ more near and more dear in the suffering than anywhere else. The nearest that I have found Him was in the midst of the hardest times of my life. I found out how real He is; I found out that He truly does fight for me; I found out that He does work all things together for my good. The miracles have flowed the most freely in the midst of the storms, when I'm weak and broken, because I know it's all Him and give Him all the glory.

I've received His presence and comfort. I have found Him as the Good Teacher, Comforter, Helper, and so much more in the midst of the suffering. And I still find Him there, time and time again. It's like He's waiting there in the suffering for me. Not that He isn't there at other times—we know He's always there—but there's a unique experience of His presence because He also walked through suffering as a man.

But remember, it's not enough to just come to Him when things are hard. We must prize this intimacy with Him at all times.

THE JOY

You *will* go through suffering; you can't avoid it. You *will* have mountains, and you *will* have valleys. But remember what King David wrote: "Though I walk through the valley of the shadow of death, I will fear no evil; for You are with me."[8] He's going to walk with you in every season.

Don't chase the calling on your life; chase Jesus. If you are chasing your calling, the moment things get hard, the moment the suffering comes, the moment you have to carry your cross, you're going to give up.

I've seen many young people give up when it got hard. They threw their cross on the ground because they wanted to accomplish their calling more than they wanted to just know Jesus. You will receive your calling first, but then the suffering will test whether you are focused on your own success or on intimacy with Him.

"Don't chase the calling on your life; chase Jesus."

Allow the Lord to carry the burdens for you by abiding in Him. If you abide in Him, you will bear fruit in every season. This abiding is the key to life. If you want to make it through the suffering, you *must* learn to abide. He is your strength and source, and He must become that—not just something we speak about, but something we live out every day. If He is truly all we live for, then even in the midst of the suffering, He will still be our number one.

It's all about Him—He is your destiny and purpose. When you stay with Him, you will end up in your purpose. If He's number one, the valleys won't stop you from fulfilling all that He has planned for your life. It's a joy when you understand this. And your joy doesn't depend on your circumstances or your calling; it's found in Him alone.

As we run the race, we don't look unto our calling —we look unto Jesus. It's a joy because He is joy, happiness, and peace. If you truly live your life for Him, you will remain at peace and at joy because your eyes are fixed on Him and not your issues. It's a joy because He's there! Wherever He is, there is joy and freedom—freedom from your worries and pain. It's a joy because there is fruit coming out of it. It's a joy because you will gain revelation, sonship, identity, fruit, and so much more. Just don't lose sight of Him.

Start now, not when it gets hard. Seek Him now. Fall on your knees and cry out to Him that you may love Him the way that you're

"He is ready and waiting for you to seek Him with all of your heart."

supposed to. He is ready and waiting for you to seek Him with all of your heart. If you try to push through using your own ability, you will find that the suffering causes you to despair and even give up. But if you realize that He wants to be your strength and your source of life, you will find joy no matter what comes your way.

"There's no other formula—Jesus is the formula."

There's no other formula; *Jesus* is the formula. So often we try to put formulas together for how to get through the wilderness step by step. But there's no formula. Everyone's wilderness, trial, test, or discipline looks different. This book hasn't given you a formula; it's an encouragement to keep your eyes fixed on Jesus. Whatever you have to do, keep your eyes on Him and follow Him. And when the world sees you walking through the storm with your head up, they will question what is different about you. Your joy will bring breakthroughs and hope to others.

People need to see someone who can withstand the fire, because your revelation then becomes their breakthrough. When you walk through it, you pioneer a way for others to walk through it also. So embrace every moment of it, looking unto Jesus.

GLOBAL REVIVAL

ABOUT THE MINISTRY

Global Revival was founded by Mark Morozov. Our prayers are to spark people's hearts to see souls saved not just locally, but also globally. We want to become a platform for the next generation. We are currently using our relationships and resources as much as possible to see the great commission be fulfilled through many different young Evangelists partnered with Global Revival. The ministry focuses on different angles to equip the global body evangelistically. Dear friend, if the body of Christ needs anything, it is to be revived and equipped to go out to save other souls. Evangelism is like an essential vitamin to the Christian. At the end of our lives we will stand before God. We will only bring ourselves and others, not any of our possessions or belongings. We sponsor and send out young evangelists. You can Join us today in spreading the Gospel of Jesus Christ prayerfully and/or financially. We are currently traveling both locally and globally seeing God move in signs and wonders!

VISION STATEMENT

Revive

In order for our generation to be activated, they first need to be revived through the preaching of the Gospel.

Disciple

We focus on discipling the people of God through biblical teaching and one on one training.

Unite

Jesus said, "a house divided against itself cannot stand." We work to unite the body of Christ in order to move the kingdom forward.

Activate

Once a disciple has been created, they need to be activated into the calling that God has on their life.

MEET THE AUTHOR

MARK MOROZOV is the Founding Director of *Global Revival*. His heart's desire is to see a generation revived by Jesus, walking in its full potential in Jesus Christ. He longs to see many people impact their own spheres of influence. Mark is a worldwide traveling Revivalist preaching Jesus Christ with powerful signs and wonders following.

 instagram.com/markmorozov

CITATIONS

1. The Reality of the Christian Life

1. Romans 8:28
2. Psalm 37:4
3. Matthew 9:37-38
4. Genesis 15:1
5. Acts 8:3
6. Acts 9:1
7. Acts 9:9
8. Acts 9:16
9. Acts 9:23
10. Acts 21:11
11. Acts 21:13
12. 2 Corinthians 12:9 (NIV)
13. 2 Corinthians 12:9-19 (NIV)
14. Mark 1-:29-30
15. Psalm 23:4 (NIV)

2. The Purpose of Suffering

1. John 10:10
2. Romans 14:17
3. Hosea 4:6
4. Hebrews 12:11
5. 2 Chronicles 32:31
6. Isaiah 40:31
7. 1 Corinthians 3:2
8. James 4:8

3. Refined by Fire

1. Joshua 1:9 (NIV)
2. Romans 15:5 (NIV)
3. Bill Johnson, "Lesson Preview: Worship in All Seasons—Worship Leading," WorshipU, Bethel Music, accessed July 15, 2020, https://app.worshipu.com/library/worship-in-all-seasons-worship-leading.
4. 1 Corinthians 10:13
5. 2 Timothy 2:21 (NASB)
6. Revelation 3:16
7. Revelation 3:18–19
8. Hebrews 12:6
9. Daniel 3:17–18
10. Proverbs 26:27
11. Daniel 3:25
12. James 1:2–3
13. 1 Peter 5:9
14. Job 1:5
15. Job 1:7
16. Job 1:8
17. Job 1:20
18. Job 1:22
19. Job 23:10

4. The Sufferings of Christ

1. Mark 1:11
2. Luke 2:41–50
3. Hebrews 5:8
4. Matthew 12:24
5. Mark 2:16
6. Matthew 14

7. Matthew 26:39
8. Matthew 26:39
9. John 11:16
10. Matthew 27:46
11. John 11:3
12. John 11:4
13. John 11:21
14. John 11:24
15. Philippians 3:10
16. Hebrews 4:15
17. Hebrews 2:18
18. Matthew 5:3–4
19. John 14:26 (KJV)
20. Isaiah 41:10
21. 1 Peter 5:7 (NIV)

5. The Aftermath

1. Nehemiah 2:19
2. Nehemiah 4:1
3. 1 Timothy 1:18
4. Proverbs 29:18 (KJV)
5. 1 Corinthians 15:19
6. Philippians 2:9
7. Romans 8:18
8. Psalm 23:4

Made in the USA
Columbia, SC
19 February 2025

54018533R00072